POEMS ABOUT PEOPLE WORKING
FOR A BETTER WORLD

# VOICES

## OF

# JUSTICE

A WHO DID IT FIRST? BOOK

Henry Holt and Company
New York

GEORGE ELLA LYON     ILLUSTRATED BY JENNIFER M. POTTER

Henry Holt and Company, *Publishers since 1866*

Henry Holt® is a registered trademark of Macmillan Publishing Group, LLC

120 Broadway, New York, NY 10271

mackids.com

Text copyright © 2020 by George Ella Lyon

Illustrations copyright © 2020 by Jennifer M. Potter

Library of Congress Cataloging-in-Publication Data is available.

ISBN 978-1-250-26320-9

Our books may be purchased in bulk for promotional, educational, or business use.

Please contact your local bookseller or the Macmillan Corporate and Premium Sales Department

at (800) 221-7945 ext. 5442 or by email at MacmillanSpecialMarkets@macmillan.com.

First edition, 2020

Book design by Mike Burroughs

The illustrations were rendered digitally and combined with textures made from gouache and pastel.

Printed in China by 1010 Printing International Limited, North Point, Hong Kong

1  3  5  7  9  10  8  6  4  2

To my granddaughter, Mina,
and to all who read this book.
We need your voices!
—G. E. L.


For Mark and Edith,
who are kind and generous . . .
especially with art supplies.
—J. M. P.

# CONTENTS

You use your voice every day—to say good morning to family and friends, to answer a question in class, or to sing. You also use your voice when you write or sign or communicate in other ways.

The people you will meet in this book knew the power of a voice and used their voices to become activists. Activists are people who work to bring about political and social change. Some of the activists in this book have used their voices to lift others up or to change people's minds. Some have spoken out for their communities, for the environment, or for the rights of animals. All of them have used their voices to fight for justice and to change the world for the better. Your voice can make a difference too! So speak up and speak out when you see injustice—the world will be a better place because you did.

# XIUHTEZCATL MARTINEZ

"Every choice we make,"
he said, "is for or against
our future." He was six,

giving his first speech,
calling out grown-ups
to save the sacred earth.

Now a young hip-hop
artist, this half-Aztec boy
carries the name Turquoise

Warrior, and he fights
for us all. Look at him!
Long hair flowing over

his suit coat, speaking
to the United Nations,
to conferences about

climate change, to TV
audiences around
the world. His message:

We owe our lives
to the land, the air,
the water. Together

we are the keepers
of life. Speak out now!

# NELSON MANDELA

On his first day of school
the white teacher told him
his tribal name would not do.
You shall be called Nelson, she said.
Neither of them dreamed that someday
he would be called *Father of a Nation*.

From tending sheep and herding cattle
in the South African hills
where he felt "free in every way,"
Mandela went off to school
and learned how bound he was
by a system called apartheid—
white laws that kept non-whites
poor and struggling.

From the boy who squabbled and played
with his eight brothers and sisters,
then shared meals with them
from the common dish,
Mandela grew into the lawyer who fought
to bring everyone to the table.

On trial for leading his people
in their demand for justice,
he declared, "It is a cause
for which . . . I am prepared to die."
The government sent him to prison for life.

But you can't lock up a movement.
Comrades on the outside continued to fight.
Like-minded people in far-away countries
joined them, chanting *Free Mandela!*
*End apartheid!*

After twenty-seven years,
the government released him.
He went right back to work.

Four years later came the first election
in which all South Africans could vote.
They chose as their president
that sheep-herding, stick-fighting boy,
the man willing to give his life
so that all could be free.

# JANE ADDAMS

A gutsy girl from a wealthy family, Jane was
motherless, and money couldn't save her from
pain in her spine. Still, after seeing the bare-bones
houses of the poor, she knew that since they had too
little, she had too much. She vowed when she was grown
she would build a big house amid the little ones. It would be
years before she knew what she wanted to create there: a place
where poor people,  many of them immigrants,  could
be fed, taught & clothed, where they found childcare,
job training, art & music. Where community happened.
Using her inheritance as a start, Jane raised money &
recruited teachers & in 1889, she opened Hull House

| | |
|---|---|
| in Chicago's slums. | She knew that no person |
| is better than anyone | else but some have better |
| chances. Jane set out | to change that by opening |
| at Hull House a door to | equality. Let's work to |

keep it

O P E N

.

# THE STUDENTS OF
# MARJORY STONEMAN DOUGLAS

It's hard not to hide when you're afraid.
After the shooting at their school
Stoneman Douglas students
were sad & scared    & angry.
They could have huddled in their houses.
Instead, they turned to one another,
took the fire of their feelings
& made a plan to change the world.

They weren't just angry
at the boy who held the gun.
They were furious at grown-ups
who had refused to pass laws
that would have kept him
from getting it.

Politicians, preachers, everyday people
sent them flowers, thoughts & prayers.
We don't want your prayers, they said.
We want your vote.

At the state capitol in Tallahassee,
they told their lawmakers,
We are your children.
You have failed us.

In Washington, DC, they did the same.
With the Peace Warriors of Chicago,
kids from a mostly African American
high school on the South Side,
where gun violence is a threat
to residents every day,
they rallied half a million people
for the March for Our Lives.
They demanded laws that limit
who gets guns & how powerful
those guns can be. Around
the country & the world,
young people marched with them.

Some lawmakers listened.
Some laws were changed.
More need changing.
Help get the word out:
#NeverAgain #EnoughisEnough

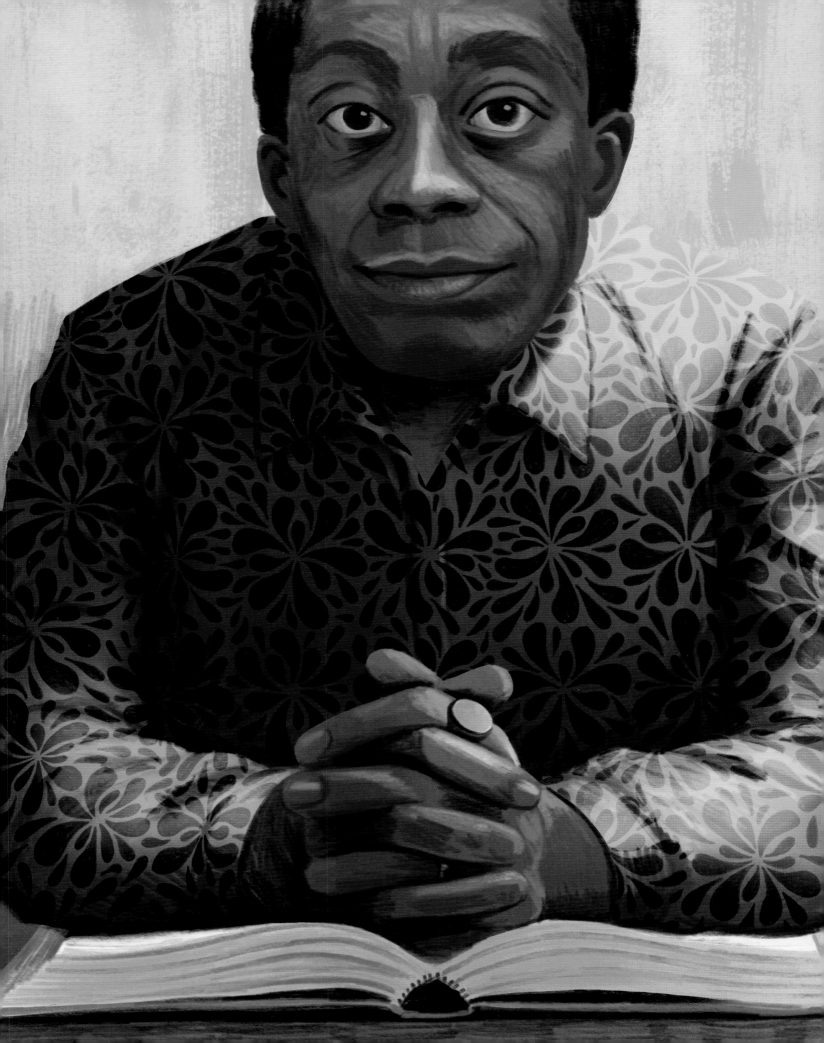

# JAMES BALDWIN

Listen! This man
means business &
his business is
the rights of every
body—every color
every gender—
to the fruits of
the Tree of Life.

He calls out lies
and hate. He speaks
truth to America
which doesn't want
to hear from him.
Too bad! He won't
take the shame white
folks try to put

on him, like he is
a beast to bear
their burdens. He
will love who he
loves & write books—
books full of what
it's like to be
a Black man pinned

to the basement
floor of a white
man's mind. He says,
You put me down
so you don't have
to look at your
ugly selves. But I
stand up. I stand

up & am free.

# VIRGINIA WOOLF

She was hungry to learn,
but it wasn't proper
for girls of her social class
to go to school, so all
her studies were at home
until she was fifteen.

Her heart was set
on being a great writer,
but everyone knew
that a girl's job

was to grow into a
mirror to show her
husband his greatness,
while (for no pay, of course)
giving birth to his children,
hosting his parties,
running his household.
Women's brains and bodies
were deemed too delicate
to do anything else.

That, Virginia said,
is how men keep
all the power!
Few women have
ever had a chance
to be writers, scholars,
artists. Until we have
a room of our own,
she declared, & money
of our own to live on,
the genius of half
the human race
will be sacrificed
to the other half.

# CHIUNE SUGIHARA

*A man is writing sixteen hours a day,*
*writing the same thing over and over:*

a transit visa, which is like a ticket
that lets people travel from one country
through others until they reach
somewhere they can be safe. Day
after day, daylight into dark

*Sugihara is writing sixteen hours a day.*

He writes quickly on official paper
changing only the names of the travelers.
He stamps the visas with the seal of Japan
though his government has told him
he must not do it.

                          They deny him

*the right to write the visas he is writing,*

the chance to save the people at his gate—
hundreds, then thousands of Polish Jews
pressed against the fence, caught in Lithuania
between Nazis to the west and Russians to the east.

*Sugihara is writing sixteen hours a day,*

though he and his family know what this
could cost them. He will lose his job,
they could all lose their lives.
But his wife, Yukiko, agrees
they must risk it, and their son,
Hiroki, says they have to help.
When Japan at last closes his office
he moves his family to a hotel where

*Sugihara is writing sixteen hours a day.*

And when he and his family must leave Lithuania
desperate people follow them to the train.

*Sugihara is writing on the platform by the tracks.*

Some recall visas handed out the train window.
Thousands of visas, many for families,
Sugihara writes in thirty-five days.

The hand of evil closes on the Jews of Europe

*but Sugihara writes and six thousand slip free.*

# THE WOMEN OF GREENHAM COMMON

We were just young mums     who didn't want our children to die
in a nuclear war.   America planned to install cruise missiles
near a sleepy town in England and citizens weren't asked
a thing about it.   We wanted to have      a voice!   We put
out a call for folks to march with us more than a hundred miles
from Cardiff, Wales, to Greenham Common, Berkshire, to deliver
a petition and demand a conversation.   On August 27, 1981,
we set out: thirty-six women, six men,     and four babies in push-chairs.

Nobody listened.   So   like Suffragettes   we chained ourselves
to the airfield's main gate.      Still no response.   We made camp
and asked other women to join us.    They came by busloads,
gathering around the fire that centered our circle. Meeting, singing,
sleeping in benders—plastic stretched over bent branches—many
of us stayed through winter. But we did more than camp.

To get our cause in the news, we cut through the fence, took over
the sentry box    danced on the silos.    Hard as the living was,
we decided we had to stay to make our leaders hear us.
We blocked gates we named for the colors of the rainbow,
lay down in front of convoys.   Police arrested us   tried us
imprisoned us   bulldozed our camp.   We sang through
it all, caring for our children, giving birth.  More women came.

In December 1982, we had thirty thousand women holding hands
around the nine-mile fence to Embrace the Base. We wove symbols
of our lives    into that fence—family photos, baby blankets, flowers,
tea kettles, toys—all the life we loved that bombs would obliterate.
We stayed for years. Across the globe, women started sister protests.

And in 1987, the US and the USSR signed a treaty: the cruise would
be gone!   Gorbachev, the Russian leader, said the peace movement
made him think differently about the arms race. Many of us left
Greenham Common then, six years after we set out for a ten-day march.
We had put our lives on the line. We had made our voices heard

and we had called      around the world      a circle for peace.

# GRETA THUNBERG

September 23, 2019

A Swedish teenager, blond
hair braided, Greta stands
straight despite the weight
of the world on her shoulders.

First she went on strike
from school for climate justice.
Then students in other
countries followed her lead.

Now at the United Nations
the eyes of world
leaders are upon her.
Greta stares right back.

"You have stolen my dreams
and my childhood,"
she tells them,
"with your empty words.

"People are suffering. People
are dying. Entire ecosystems
are collapsing, and all you
can talk about

"is money and fairy tales
of eternal economic growth.
For thirty years, the science
has been crystal clear.

"How dare you
continue to look away?"

# JEANNETTE RANKIN

*(The bolded words are Jeannette's own.)*

| | |
|---|---|
| **You** | ! Imagine the courage— |
| **can** | you?  To vote— |
| **no** | when President Woodrow Wilson calls for war? Even |
| **more** | —imagine that you, as the first woman in the US Congress, need to |
| **win** | approval from congressmen who had even made an issue of |
| **a** | hat: Should you be allowed to wear it in the chambers? Now |
| **war** | was the question, and you said *No*. Still, this vote was worlds easier |
| **than** | 1941's would be. Fifty-five men stood with |
| **you** | against entering the Great War. But the day after Pearl Harbor: |
| **can** | you imagine standing alone against FDR's demand for war, only to |
| **win** | hisses and a mob which chased you into |
| **an** | empty phone booth where you called the police at the edge of an |
| **earthquake**. | ? |

# THE TRIMATES

## JANE GOODALL
## DIAN FOSSEY
## BIRUTÉ GALDIKAS

WHOLE ROU

and
the
us
will save
That's what
orangutans,
Gorillas
chimpanzees
will save
That's what
*
money.
not
power,
not
—*life*
for
must be
love
our
creatures
wild
that to save
clear
work makes
The Trimates'
*
labor on.
and Galdikas
Goodall
continues.
her legacy
has died,
Though Fossey
*
habitats too.
but their
of the primates
not only
the rescue
to support
money
to raise
speeches
They gave
homelands.
and their
creatures
of these
of the beauty

WORLD.

Three young women set out across the world to Tanzania Rwanda Borneo to learn all they could about chimpanzees gorillas orangutans.

*

They hiked climbed and waded through rain forests mountains swamps watching mapping reaching, discovering teaching fighting for the lives of the primates who cannot survive unless their habitats thrive too.

*

These three scientists shared a mentor, Louis Leakey, who called them the Trimates.

*

And try they did! Not only in the field. They wrote about their findings to give people

# ALEXYA SALVADOR

From the time she was born,
they told Alexya she was a boy,
but inside she knew she was a girl.
She was bullied, beaten up.

Once she was grown, she learned
        her outside and inside selves could match!
People in the market laughed,
        made fun of her, turned away.
                Alexya went home and cried.

                But she knew she didn't want
        to hide.
                Besides
                she was almost six feet tall!

So Alexya made herself strong
                                inside.

        "Let them say whatever they want," she told herself.
                                *I am who I am.*

Who she is now is a pastor—
the first transgender one in Brazil.
        Teacher, wife, mother
                                of three children,
                                two of them trans.
        Her daughter Ana had longed for
                "a family
                        who accepts me
                                for who I am."

        That family was Alexya's.

        Asked about her mom, Ana says,

        "I love her to the size of the world."

# JULIA BUTTERFLY HILL

Do you like to climb trees?
Would you live in one
for two years to save its life?
Julia Butterfly Hill did.
She camped near the top
of a thousand-year-old redwood
named Luna, who was old
when Columbus misclaimed America.

After a car wreck almost
killed her, Julia went west
searching for work that meant
more than money. She found it
in California's redwood forest
where Earth First and other activists
were trying to save the ancient trees.

Surely loggers wouldn't cut down
a tree that someone lived in!
So on December 10, 1997,
Julia climbed up a hundred and eighty feet
and made Luna her home.

Pacific Lumber tried
to scare her out

      with a helicopter hovering
   churning the air        its lights so bright she couldn't sleep.
They tried to starve her out
    turning back Earth First friends    who were bringing her food.
They tried to break her down
     as they shouted
      how they'd hurt Julia when she surrendered.

She stayed strong
and called for protests around the world.
Money and pledges of support poured in.

Pacific Lumber had to cut a deal
instead of a tree.

After 738 days Julia came down,
kissed the ground at Luna's roots
and cried.

# SHIRLEY CHISHOLM

Until 1968, no Black woman
had ever been elected
to the US Congress.

> Way past due.
> Let her through.
> Here comes Shirley Chisholm.

Until 1969, no newcomer
in Congress had ever said *No*
to their committee assignment.

> Open the door.
> Hold the floor.
> Here comes Shirley Chisholm.

Until 1972, only one woman
had run for president of the US
and she was white.

> Never mind.
> It's about time.
> Here comes Shirley Chisholm.

> She knows she won't win.
> She does it to begin
> a path for women who'll come after.

> Unbossed and unbought
> that's how Shirley fought.
> That's what Shirley taught
> with integrity and laughter.

# CRISTINA JIMÉNEZ

If you are in the United States
but don't have papers that        say
you belong in the United States
you are in danger of being        kicked out,

sent back to a situation
you may not remember              that made
the home you loved                dangerous.
So you hide. You keep

out of the light of               belonging,
of community, because of          fear,
fear you wear like clothes.
Cristina knows. She               arrived

in the US at thirteen
from Ecuador. Her parents         left
their country, their language,    to build
a better life for their           children.

Cristina is devoting her          self
to building a brighter            future
for others like her.              It starts with

        making a safe circle
      where young people gather
          to share their stories,
      to fight for immigrant rights

        so that Dreamers can stay
          and work to become
        part of their new country.
                Cristina

is making               doors               in the walls

                that divide

                    us.

# JASILYN CHARGER

She ran to save    the life of her people

from the oil pipeline    they called the Black Snake

It was to be built    beneath their land and river

If the Snake's skin split    oil would poison their water

            Mni Wiconi    water is life

Five hundred miles    she ran with her people

Campbell, North Dakota    to Omaha, Nebraska

When no official    in the Army Corps would listen

they ran all the way    to Washington, DC

Twelve hundred miles    to carry their petition

twelve hundred miles    to stop the Black Snake

Then Jasilyn called    the youth of Indian country

to join her in prayer    at Sacred Stone Camp

She knew they were the ones    their ancestors dreamed of

They must stand at Standing Rock    for the water, the earth.

# YOU!

So new
so unlike anyone
who has come before.

Oh, you may have
one parent's eyes,
another's laugh,
may walk like your grandfather,
hold your hands like your grandmother
                                    just        so.
Or your family may be one
not made by birth.
Then      love teaches you
to move like one, speak      like another.

                    It gladdens grown-ups
                    to see themselves in you.

But you yourself—you are new
and you bring gifts
the human family
has been waiting for.

How will you
discover your gifts?
How will you
give them a voice?

In these poems, you've met people
who grew into big voices.
Yours doesn't have to be big.
It just has to be yours.

You              so new
in this old, old world:
Welcome!

# MORE ABOUT THE ACTIVISTS

### XIUHTEZCATL MARTINEZ (2000–)

Indigenous activist and hip-hop artist Xiuhtezcatl Martinez has been calling for action to stop climate change since he was six years old. Growing up in Boulder, Colorado, he learned the Mashika (Aztec) reverence for the sacred earth from his father, and the scientific evidence of how we are endangering it from his mother. Because of his knowledge, eloquence, and courage, Xiuhtezcatl has been invited to speak at many gatherings, including the United Nations and the World Conference on Climate Change. He is youth director of Earth Guardians, an organization that trains young people to be leaders in the movement for a healthier planet and a more just society. In 2015, Earth Guardians joined twenty-one other young people in a lawsuit against the US government for failing to protect our planet from global warming. Their case is still in court.

### NELSON MANDELA (1918–2013)

Nelson Mandela was born on the Eastern Cape of South Africa. His father was a minor chief, and Mandela was raised to be part of the king's council. When he learned that a marriage had been arranged for him, he escaped to Johannesburg, where he saw firsthand the desperate conditions for living and working that white rulers of his country imposed on everybody else. He became a lawyer to defend his people in court and joined the African National Conference to give Black South Africans a political voice. His leadership in the fight to end apartheid landed him in prison for life, but it also brought international attention to the struggle. Released in 1990, Mandela helped secure the right to vote for all citizens, regardless of color, and in 1994, he became the first Black president of his country, forging a way forward for his warring nation through forgiveness and reconciliation.

Quotation source: *Mandela: Son of Africa, Father of a Nation*. Produced by Jonathan Demme (Palm Pictures, 1996). https://www.youtube.com/watch?v=0_eYnCrh6gU&t=430s

### JANE ADDAMS (1860–1935)

Born to a wealthy family in Illinois, Jane Addams was the eighth of nine children. Motherless at age three, then stricken as a small child with a spinal disease, she knew emotional and physical pain from an early age. This made her aware of difficulties in other peoples' lives. When she saw the suffering that poverty brings, she told her father, "When I grow up, I will have a large house, but it will not be built among the other large houses, but right in the midst" of the poor. In 1889, Addams fulfilled that vow, cofounding Hull House in the Chicago slums, where the poor were fed, taught, and given access to the arts by teachers who shared Jane's vision of a more equitable society. Through Hull House, she helped launch the settlement movement in America and invented what we call social work. Years later, as the horrors of the First World War became evident, Addams began working with women in Europe and the United Kingdom to find pathways to peace. In 1931, she was the first woman to win the Nobel Peace Prize.

### THE STUDENTS OF MARJORY STONEMAN DOUGLAS HIGH SCHOOL

In the aftermath of a 2018 shooting at their school in Parkland, Florida, students came together to call out adults for not passing strict gun control laws that could have protected them. After taking their message to the state capital, they partnered with Peace Warriors, who were from a mostly African American high school in Chicago, and called for a national March for Our Lives. More than two hundred thousand people joined them in Washington, DC, and sister marches were held around the world. From that foundation, Parkland students, and people of all ages inspired by them, have worked to change how we talk about gun violence in the US and how we regulate guns. Sixty-seven gun safety bills were passed in 2018 alone; many banks and businesses broke their connections to the National Rifle Association; and a huge increase in turnout among young voters helped elect officials who vowed to fight for gun safety.

## JAMES BALDWIN (1924–1987)

James Baldwin was born in New York City's Harlem, the son of a Pentecostal preacher. As a teenager, Baldwin himself tried preaching, but he soon turned his passion for language and his dream of a better world to a life of writing and speaking. As a gay Black man, Baldwin found his choices so restricted in his own country that he lived much of his life in Paris, where he continued his fight for civil and gay rights. He said that from the other side of the ocean, he could see where he came from: "I am the grandson of a slave, and I am a writer. I must deal with both." In novels such as *Giovanni's Room* and essay collections such as *Notes of a Native Son* and *The Fire Next Time*, Baldwin exposed white people's need to create a false idea of blackness so they could justify their racist actions.

Quotation source: Bennetts, Leslie. "James Baldwin Reflects on 'Go Tell It' PBS Film." *The New York Times*, January 10, 1985

## VIRGINIA WOOLF (1882–1941)

Born into a well-to-do literary family, Virginia Woolf was the seventh child in her parents' blended household. She is known for the ways her method of storytelling helped shape the modern novel. To devote her life to writing, Woolf had to defy expectations of her family and her social class that said her chief goals in life were to be beautiful, marry well, be a gracious, hospitable wife to an important man, and bear his children. With her older sister, Vanessa, an artist, Woolf turned her back on that world and centered her life around reading and writing essays, novels, biography, letters, and diaries. In all her work, from her first novel, *The Voyage Out*, through her masterpiece, *To the Lighthouse*, to her final novel, *Between the Acts*, Virginia's radical writing captures and questions life as she experienced it. In *A Room of One's Own*, she explores how society limits women's opportunities—particularly women writers—while it gives men better education, better choices, and more money. In *Three Guineas*, Woolf declares, "As a woman I have no country. As a woman I want no country. As a woman my country is the whole world."

Quotation source: Woolf, Virginia. *Three Guineas*. Hogarth Press, 1938.

## CHINUE SUGIHARA (1900–1986)

When Sugihara was born in Kozuchi Town, Japan, his father worked in a tax office, and the family lived in a borrowed Buddhist temple. In his early years, as his father was transferred, Sugihara and his family moved many times. Perhaps these multiple moves influenced his decision to go into the Foreign Ministry when he grew up. Perhaps,

too, it gave him greater sympathy for the refugees who came to his office when he was vice-consul in Lithuania and Jews were on the run from Nazis in 1939 on the eve of World War II. They needed official papers to get them across borders to a safe place, and they begged for Sugihara's help. Though his bosses refused permission, Sugihara chose to do it anyway. Different sources give different numbers, but it is safe to say that in his marathon of writing transit visas, Sugihara saved thousands of Jewish refugees. In 1985, the Israeli organization Yad Vashem recognized him as Righteous Among Nations.

## THE WOMEN OF GREENHAM COMMON

In 1981, NATO announced that nuclear missiles would be deployed at a base in rural Berkshire, United Kingdom. Horrified at the prospect of nuclear war, Ann Pettitt and three other young mothers formed Women for Life on Earth and organized a march from Cardiff to the military base to demand public debate. Ten days and a hundred and ten miles later, some of the protesters chained themselves to the Royal Air Force gate. Getting no response, some marchers resolved to stay until their petition was recognized and the issue was open for discussion. Many women joined them. For almost two decades, the Women of Greenham Common kept the missile question in the news by lying in front of trucks, cutting the fence, occupying the air traffic control tower, and dancing on the silos. Arrested, fined, and imprisoned, they called for women around the world to join them. In December 1982, during Embrace the Base, thirty thousand women held hands around the nine-mile perimeter fence. Women remained in substantial numbers till the first cruise missiles were removed because of the INF treaty in 1987. They seeded a global peace movement which helped end the Cold War. (As of this writing, President Trump has taken the US out of that treaty.)

## GRETA THUNBERG (2003–)

A Swedish climate activist, Greta Thunberg was only fifteen when she sat in front of parliament in Stockholm with a sign that read *School Strike for Climate*. Greta said it did no good for her to be in school while adults refused to do something about global warming, which threatens all life. Her action led to Fridays for Future, a worldwide student protest. Over eleven million people have marched in response to her call. She has spoken at international gatherings, including the 2019 United Nations climate summit, where she told those in power, "For more than thirty years, the science has been crystal clear. How dare you continue to look away?"

Quotation source: *PBS NewsHour*, September 23, 2019.
https://www.youtube.com/watch?v=KAJsdgTPJpU

### DOLORES HUERTA (1930–)

Raised by a single mother in Stockton, California, Dolores Huerta learned early about the struggles of low-wage workers. Her mother, a hotel owner, gave farm-worker families affordable rooms; sometimes she even let them stay for free. Being Mexican American, Huerta couldn't miss the link between having brown skin and being poor. When she was grown and a mother herself, she worked as a teacher until she volunteered to go door-to-door to register voters and saw the terrible conditions farm workers and their families were living in. Determined to help change this, Huerta quit her job and became a labor organizer. With César Chávez, she founded United Farm Workers so that people could have collective power to fight for better wages, working conditions, and health care. Using rallies, picket lines, headlines, and solidarity, the UFW affected change for the workers, including higher wages and better medical care. The mother of eleven children, Huerta continues to work for equality and justice through the Dolores Huerta Foundation.

### JEANNETTE RANKIN (1880–1973)

Born in Montana, Jeannette Rankin was a pacifist and a fierce fighter for women's right to vote. In 1916, she became the first woman elected to Congress in the United States. True to her belief that war only creates economic and personal destruction that leads to more war, she voted against US entry into both World War I and World War II. That last vote ended her political career, but not her activism. At age eighty-seven, she led the Jeannette Rankin Brigade in the 1968 March on Washington opposing the Vietnam War. A scholarship fund she established still helps older low-income women attend college.

Quotation source: "The Women of the 116th Congress Will Make a Difference by Being Different," by Colman McCarthy. *National Catholic Reporter*, January 19, 2019. https://www.ncronline.org/news/opinion/its-happening/women-116th-Congress-will-make-difference-being-different

### JANE GOODALL (1934–)

As a little girl growing up in London (United Kingdom), Goodall was given a stuffed animal chimpanzee named Jubilee. Her love of animals started there. A little older, she read the *Tarzan* books, and imagined going to Africa to live with wild creatures. Hard work, a supportive family, and a little luck made that dream come true. Mentored by Louis Leakey, Goodall became a primatologist and spent fifty-five years studying chimpanzees in the Gombe Stream National Park in Tanzania. Now, through the Jane Goodall Institute, she travels the world to teach about the need to save chimpanzees and the natural world that sustains us all. Through this work, Goodall discovered that young people were weighed down by despair because they felt they could do nothing to save the dying planet. To help them find their own power, Goodall founded Roots & Shoots, a program that guides young people in making a difference for the environment, for animals, and for their community. There are now over seven thousand groups in fifty countries. Goodall says, "Each one of us makes a difference . . . and we have a choice as to what difference we make."

Quotation Source: "5 Minutes of Wisdom with Dr. Jane Goodall." *YouTube*, uploaded by IFOAM – Organics International, February 13, 2020. https://www.youtube.com/watch?time_continue=241&v=W0IcPsElaQc

### DIAN FOSSEY (1932–1985)

Born in Northern California, Dian Fossey grew up with a love of animals, especially horses, and was on her high school's riding team. She was working as an occupational therapist when she felt called to go to Africa after a friend showed her photos from a recent trip. It was there in 1963 that she met Dr. Louis Leakey, learned of Jane Goodall's work, and saw her first mountain gorilla. Fossey returned in 1966 and began the study of these gorillas that would be her life's work. Because these great apes were threatened by poachers (who killed them for trophies and meat) and by destruction of their forest home, Fossey raised money to protect mountain gorillas and their habitat. The Dian Fossey Gorilla Fund International continues her work.

### BIRUTÉ GALDIKAS (1946–)

Born in Germany to Lithuanian refugee parents, Biruté Galdikas moved to Canada when she was two. The first library book she checked out was *Curious George*. Later she read about Dian Fossey's and Jane Goodall's work in *National Geographic*, and was captivated by their stories and images. As a graduate student in California, Galdikas met Dr. Louis Leakey who, with help from *National Geographic*, assisted her in setting up a research center in Borneo to study orangutans. In addition to observing and teaching about these primates, Galdikas learned a great deal about the rain forest and the many forms of life it shelters. She created a rehabilitation center for orangutans that had been orphaned or illegally sold as pets. Like Fossey and Goodall, Galdikas has had to defend against destruction of the habitat her primates require to live. Through the Orangutan Foundation International, she is still working to ensure their survival.

## ALEXYA SALVADOR (1981–)

Born near São Paulo, Brazil, Alexya Salvador didn't feel at home in her body as a child. People told her she was a boy, but boys didn't accept her. She wanted to play with girl cousins, but that wasn't allowed. It was very confusing! Until she was twenty-eight years old, she identified as a gay man. But that didn't feel true, either. Finally, she realized she was a woman. When she found out she could have a body that matched who she was on the inside, she saw hope for a true life at last. Now Salvador is the first transgender teacher, pastor, and adoptive parent in her country. As vice president of the Brazilian Association of Homotransaffective Families, she brings people together for conversations about the many shapes a family can take and talks about the need for LGBTI people to have a voice in politics. Now a reverend in the Metropolitan Community Church International, she preaches God's inclusive love and "every human being's right to be."

Quotation source: *Alexya*, a film by Renata Matarazzo. https://www.youtube.com/watch?v=PRFoLRplkQ8

## JULIA BUTTERFLY HILL (1974–)

Julia Butterfly Hill is an environmental activist, artist, and writer. Until she was ten, she lived with her parents and two brothers in a camper. Once, when they were hiking, a butterfly landed on her finger and stayed there the rest of the hike, giving seven-year-old Julia her nickname: Butterfly. When she was twenty-two, she was in a near-fatal car wreck. After she recovered the ability to walk and talk, she realized she wanted to do something that would make a difference. Her quest led her to California. A group called Earth First asked for a volunteer to sit in a tree named Luna for one day on a platform one hundred eighty feet off the ground; Hill was the only person who held up a hand. Little did she know she would make her home in that one-thousand-year-old tree for two years, from 1997 to 1999, to keep Pacific Lumber from cutting it down. Supported by organizations such as Earth First, she used a solar cell phone to get news out to people all over the world about what was happening to these trees and what the living earth would lose when they were gone. Ever since she climbed down, Hill has been working for environmental and social justice.

## SHIRLEY CHISHOLM (1924–2005)

Born in Brooklyn, the child of immigrants, Shirley Chisholm grew up knowing the hardships of working-class families. Once, when times were tough, she and her two younger sisters were sent to live with their grandmother on the island of Barbados. She treasured her grandmother's gifts of strength, dignity, and love. "I learned that I was somebody," Chisholm said. Her belief that this was true for *everybody* is part of what led her to run for public office. After serving in the New York legislature, she became the first African American woman elected to Congress. There she fought for the rights of the poor, for racial and gender equality, and against the Vietnam War. In 1972, she ran for president, the first African American candidate from a major party. Her slogan was "Unbought and Unbossed."

## CRISTINA JIMÉNEZ (1984–)

Cristina Jiménez came to the United States from Ecuador with her parents when she was thirteen. Like many undocumented immigrants, she grew up afraid that she or someone else in her family would be found out and deported. She couldn't get a Social Security card or a job that required one, because she wasn't a United States citizen. She couldn't apply to colleges because she'd have to reveal that she was undocumented, putting herself and her family in danger. Knowing firsthand how this situation isolates people and keeps them on the edges of society, Jiménez decided to work to change it. She began as a youth leader and eventually cofounded United We Dream, an organization that advocates for immigrants' rights. Through UWD, she helped influence President Obama to create the Deferred Action for Childhood Arrivals (DACA), a policy that extends the time young undocumented immigrants can study and work in the US. They are often called Dreamers.

## JASILYN CHARGER (1996–)

Indigenous earth activist Jasilyn Charger grew up on the Cheyenne River Reservation in South Dakota, where poverty and harsh conditions continue the persecution of Native Americans. After battling her own issues and moving away for a short time, she came home to fight for her people and her land. Her first action was to protest the proposed Keystone XL Pipeline. In April 2016, Jasilyn began living at Sacred Stone Resistance Camp on the Standing Rock Reservation to oppose the Dakota Pipeline, which would destroy sites sacred to native people and threaten their water supply. With ReZpect Our Water, an indigenous youth group, she helped organize runs to Omaha, Nebraska, and Washington, DC, to carry protest and petitions to those in power. Jasilyn also created an International Indigenous Youth Council to bring young people from many tribes together so they could make their voices heard. Jasilyn says, "Activism and spirituality live hand in hand.... We walk every day in a sacred way. Standing Rock. . . was the starting point of the road that has become my life."

Quotation source: "Jasilyn: Activist of the Land." *YouTube*, uploaded by Levi's, March 7, 2018. https://www.youtube.com/watch?v=nzXaK3gT8Ww

# A GUIDE FOR PARENTS AND CAREGIVERS

*Voices of Justice* introduces readers to a range of social justice issues and the leaders at the forefront of these movements. This book is recommended for late elementary and middle school age children; however, we encourage you to use your judgment and discretion around the readiness of your child to engage with some of the more difficult topics introduced. Factors to consider include your child's temperament and developmental level, and their current understanding. For some children, these topics may be very familiar and even a part of their lived experience. For others, their awareness may be emerging.

Invite discussion with your child around the issues introduced, providing a safe and supportive space for your child to ask questions and to share their thoughts and feelings. Below are some additional suggestions on how to facilitate these conversations:

- For younger children: Keep the narrative simple. Focus on the positive values that the activists exemplify. Validate your child's feelings. When appropriate, emphasize their safety and all the people in their lives and community who work hard to keep them safe.

- For older children: Ask them what they already know or understand about the issue. Help them process different feelings and reactions that emerge for them. Discuss your child's and family's values and ways they can live those values day to day.

- For adolescents: Explore feelings and beliefs around these issues together with your child. Talk about different ways to be involved, volunteer, or raise awareness as they feel called to action. Discuss ways to live in alignment with their values, and model this practice for and with your child.

Guide written by Dr. Danielle Vrieze, PhD, LP, child psychologist and assistant professor at University of Minnesota Medical School

# GLOSSARY

In *Voices of Justice*, you've met a number of activists, people who fought or are fighting to bring about political and social change. Activism can take many forms. Below are definitions of some kinds of activism and other important words and phrases to know.

**Advocate**—A person who publicly supports a particular cause or issue.

**Animal Rights**—The belief that animals deserve lives free from human-caused suffering. Animal rights activists, like the Trimates, fight for things such as no experiments on animals and not using animals for food, clothing, medicine, hard labor, or entertainment purposes.

**Apartheid**—A government-enforced system of racial segregation that existed in South Africa from 1948 until the early 1990s. Apartheid separated people based on the color of their skin and severely limited the rights of nonwhites. Nelson Mandela fought to end apartheid and became the first Black president of South Africa.

**Civil Rights**—Rights which belong to all citizens. Some examples of civil rights are the right to vote, the right to a public education, and the right to a fair trial. Civil rights activists fight to ensure that people aren't discriminated against based on their race, gender, sexual orientation, age, religion, and more.

**Climate Movement**—Activism related to climate change. Greta Thunberg uses her voice to call on everyone to reduce their reliance on fossil fuels (things like petroleum, coal, and natural gas, which contribute to the climate crisis). She also asks politicians and other decision-makers to listen to scientists, who agree that the Earth is warming.

**Cold War**—The period of tension and hostility between the former Soviet Union (and its allies) and the United States (and its allies). The Cold War lasted roughly from 1945 to 1990. It was called a "cold" war because both sides were afraid to fight each other directly (as opposed to a "hot" war, in which there is actual combat).

**Environmentalism**—A movement that seeks to protect, repair, and improve the health of our planet, as well as prevent future damage. Xiuhtezcatl Martinez is a vocal environmentalist who has spoken out against pesticides and fracking. Jasilyn Charger is another environmentalist. She spoke up to protect the water supply for her community.

**Human Rights**—Rights belonging to all human beings, including the right to life, freedom from slavery, freedom of opinion, and many more.

**Immigrant**—Someone who comes to a country to live permanently.

**Immigrants' Rights Movement**—A movement that seeks to protect the civil liberties (like freedom of speech and religion) and civil rights of everyone, no matter their immigration status. (Immigration status can include citizen, green card holder, refugee, and undocumented person, among others). Cristina Jiménez uses her voice to fight for immigrants' rights.

**Indigenous Rights**—Indigenous people (also known as first, native, or aboriginal people) are ethnic groups who are the original caretakers of a given region. Their rights include basic human rights but also the preservation of their land, language, religion, and other elements of their cultural heritage. Both Xiuhtezcatl Martinez (rooted in the Aztec tradition) and Jasilyn Charger (of the Cheyenne River Sioux Tribe) are activists for indigenous rights.

**LGBTQIA+ Rights Movement**—The lesbian, gay, bisexual, transgender, queer or questioning, intersex, and asexual or allied (LGBTQIA+) movement seeks to protect the rights of people who could be described by these terms. James Baldwin wrote and spoke about these rights. Alexya Salvador fights for them today in Brazil.

**Settlement House Movement**—A movement that began in the United States and England in the 1880s. The movement sought to bring rich and poor people together to provide social and educational opportunities for working-class people, many of them women and many of them immigrants. Jane Addams's Hull House was one of the first settlement houses in the US.

**Transgender**—A term for people whose gender identity (how you feel, be it girl, boy, or non-binary) is different than the sex (male or female) doctors assigned to them at birth.

**Women's Rights Movement**—A movement that aims to ensure human rights for girls and women everywhere. This movement also fights for women's health issues and equal pay. All of the women featured in this book used their voices for women's rights.

# SELECTED SOURCES

*Carry Greenham Home*. Directed by Beeban Kidron and Amanda Richardson. 1983. Beaconsfield, Buckinghamshire, England: National Film and Television School. Film. https://vimeo.com/ondemand/carrygreenhamhome.

*Chisholm '72: Unbought & Unbossed*. Directed by Shola Lynch, 2004. Realside Productions. Film. https://www.justwatch.com/us/movie/chisholm-72-unbought-and-unbossed.

"Cristina Jiménez Moreta: Social Justice Organizer." MacArthur Foundation. https://www.macfound.org/fellows/989/.

*Dolores*. Directed by Peter Bratt. 2017. Los Angeles, CA: 5 Stick Films. Film. Aired on PBS Independent Lens, 2018. https://www.pbslearningmedia.org/collection/dolores-huerta/.

"From Keystone XL Pipeline to #DAPL: Jasilyn Charger, Water Protector from Cheyenne River Reservation." Posted by Democracy Now!, January 6, 2017. YouTube video, 33:15. https://www.youtube.com/watch?v=mCQPszxc5yM.

History.com Editors. "Teen gunman kills 17, injures 17 at Parkland, Florida high school." *History*, February 6, 2019. https://www.history.com/this-day-in-history/parkland-marjory-stoneman-douglas-school-shooting.

*I Am Not Your Negro*. Directed by Raoul Peck. 2017. New York, NY: Velvet Film. Film.

"Jane Addams." Americans Who Tell the Truth. https://www.americanswhotellthetruth.org/portraits/jane-addams.

March for Our Lives. https://marchforourlives.com.

"Part 1 – Julia Butterfly Hill – Adventures in Treesitting." Posted by michaelofthemountain, January 9, 2009. YouTube video, 9:58. https://www.youtube.com/watch?v=FyLiOnmBZLw.

Robertson, Josh. "The Trimates." *Conservation Conversation*, January 10, 2017. https://www.conservationconversation.co.uk/copy-of-what-is-conservation.

Wolpe, David. "The Japanese Man Who Saved 6,000 Jews With His Handwriting," *New York Times*, October 15, 2018. https://www.nytimes.com/2018/10/15/opinion/sugihara-moral-heroism-refugees.html.

*Women of Impact*. Directed by Lisa Feit. 2019. National Geographic. Film.

Woolf, Virginia. *A Room of One's Own*. Hogarth Press, 1929; Harcourt, Brace, and World, 1957.

"Xiuhtezcatl on the Global Climate Strike," *Amanpour & Co.*, PBS, September 19, 2019. http://www.pbs.org/wnet/amanpour-and-company/video/xiuhtezcatl-martinez-on-the-global-climate-strike/.

---

## Acknowledgments for VOICES OF JUSTICE

My thanks to the many people who made this book possible:
my family
my agent, Brenda Bowen
my editor, Christian Trimmer
all the Holt team
illustrator, Jennifer M. Potter
my writing sisters
and Dick Jackson, who believed in me from the beginning.